S0-AGI-482

THE GAME PLAN

A Kids'
Musical about
God's Master Plan for Each of Us

Created by Tim Conrad
Arranged by Jukka Palonen

Performance time: 43 minutes

li**f**enas**kids**

Copyright © 2009 by Pilot Point Music, Box 419527, Kansas City, MO 64141.
All rights reserved. Litho in U.S.A.

All scripture quotations are from the *Holy Bible, New International Version®* (NIV®). Copyright © 1973, 1978, 1984 by International Bible Society. Used by permission of Zondervan Publishing House. All rights reserved.

LillenasKids.com

Contents

Kailey (me)

Kailey (me)

Kailey (me)

"Cast"

WYATT ANDERSON: 6th grade boy and lead soccer player. He struggles with taking a back seat and following God's plan at times.

ANTHONY SCALETTI: 5th grade boy and a new comer to the town and team. His parents may be divorcing.

NOAH BENJAMIN: 4th grade boy who is very precocious; looks up to Wyatt.

KATANA JOHNSON: 5th grade girl on the team who is fast and loves to read.

SADIE GRESHAM: 6th grade girl and Captain of the Cheer Squad. She struggles with rejection and maintaining a Christian attitude.

KAILEY RATCLIFF: 5th grade girl cheerleader and one of Sadie's best friends. She falls victim to peer pressure, but turns things around in the end.

COACH CALHOUN: 40s to 50s enthusiastic male coach of the Tigers who also teaches Sunday School at the church. Loves to encourage the kids in both teamwork and Christ-likeness.

JEN GORDON: Young Adult Cheer coach who helps Sadie work through her problems.

CHEERLEADER 1

CHEERLEADER 2

REFEREE

EXTRAS: Players on the Tigers, Cardinals and Cheerleaders.

Game Plan

Words and Music by
SARAH MOORE
Arr. by Jukka Palonen

(Lights up on Choir and Cast)

We want vic-to-ry; God's got a

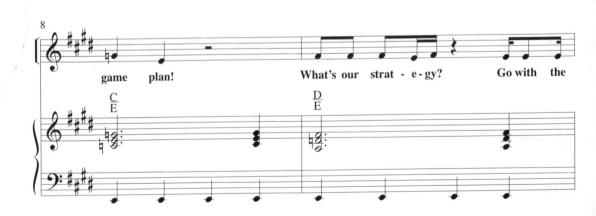

game plan! What's our strat-e-gy? Go with the

Copyright © 2009 by Pilot Point Music (ASCAP). All rights reserved.
Administered by The Copyright Company, PO Box 128139, Nashville, TN 37212-8139.

PLEASE NOTE: Copying of this product is NOT covered by CCLI licenses. For CCLI information call 1-800-234-2446.

game plan!   We want vic - to-ry;   God's got a

CD: 3 *1st time*
CD: 5 *2nd time*

game   plan!   What's our strat - e - gy?   Go with the

SOLO 1

We each have dif -f'rent strengths,   we

game   plan!

CD: 6

Prac - tice hard and play to win each and__ ev - 'ry day!

CHOIR *unis.*

We want vic - to - ry; God's got a game plan!

What's our strat - e - gy? Go with the game plan!

We want vic - to - ry; God's got a game plan!

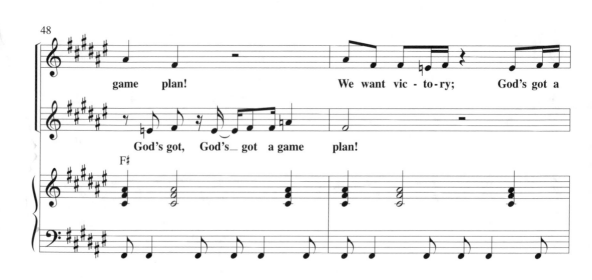

Scene One

(As song ends, lights down on choir and lights up on cast. Scene opens with main characters practicing. WYATT *and* ANTHONY *are working on headers.* KATANA *and* NOAH *are working on shielding the ball.* SADIE *and* KAILEY, *with help from others, are working on a thigh stand.* KIDS *are talking and enjoying practice.* COACH *blows his whistle and calls everyone in.)*

COACH: Hey guys, good practice today. Wyatt, you really did well on those headers. And Anthony, you served those balls to Wyatt just right! If we do that on Saturday, we should be able to improve that area of our game.

WYATT & ANTHONY: Thanks, Coach.

COACH: Noah, you and Katana really looked solid on that ball possession work, and from what I saw from Sadie and Kailey, and the cheerleaders, their cheer stunts were coming along. In fact, every one of you was showing the strengths that God put in you. If we use those strengths, and follow a good game plan, I know we have a chance to beat the Cardinals.

*(*NOAH *starts whispering to* ANTHONY.)*

WYATT: Hey, Coach!

COACH: Yes, Wyatt?

WYATT: Coach, that's like the Bible story of Moses you told us about at church last Sunday.

COACH: That's right Wyatt. *(Trying to get* NOAH'S *attention)* Noah! You were there. Do you remember what I said about Moses' strengths and where they came from?

NOAH: Yeah! God made Moses with special abilities and powers - dude, he was like Superman! *(Jumps to his feet)* Look! Up in the sky . . . it's a bird, it's a plane, - its Moses!

(KIDS laugh)

COACH: Well, sort of right, Noah. What's fascinating about the Moses story is that it shows us when God created us; He put special talents in all of us. *(Turns to* WYATT*)* Wyatt, you jump well and are good in the air. *(Turns to* KATANA*)* Katana, you're fast and can catch up to any team on a breakaway. Each one of you is an important player on that field. Like a V.I.P., you are important to the team.

KATANA: What's a V.I.P?

NOAH *(boastful)*: Coach, you mean, I'm a very important player?

COACH: Yes, Noah, you are an important player, but more importantly . . . you are a very important person to God . . . *(with a chuckle)* you're unique! In fact, every aspect of who you are was planned right down to the color of your hair and the smile on your face! He made you just the way He wanted- He made your DNA!

(Lights up on choir and music begins.)

D N A

Words and Music by
SARAH MOORE and
TIM CONRAD
Arr. by Jukka Palonen

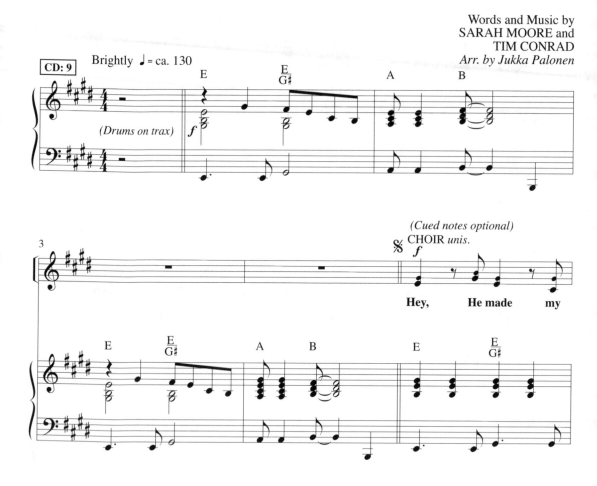

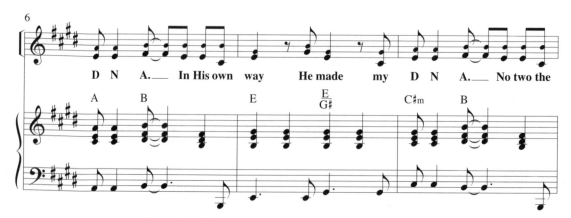

Copyright © 2009 by Pilot Point Music (ASCAP). All rights reserved.
Administered by The Copyright Company, PO Box 128139, Nashville, TN 37212-8139.

PLEASE NOTE: Copying of this product is NOT covered by CCLI licenses. For CCLI information call 1-800-234-2446.

CD: 13

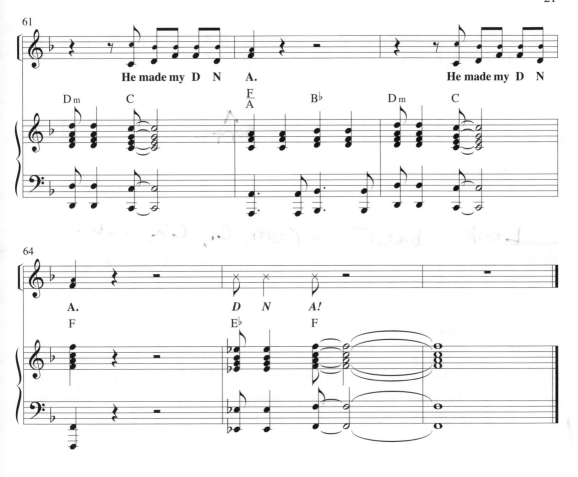

He made my D N A. He made my D N

A. D N A!

Scene Two

(Song ends. Lights down on choir and lights up on cast.)

COACH: OK, you unique V.I.P.'s. Your parents are going to be here any minute. Grab the cones and bag up the balls. *(NOAH makes a cape out of the ball bag and pretends to fly like Superman.)* Noah, Noah, come on. Pack it up.

(As team packs and leaves, JEN moves over and has a conversation with COACH away from kids. SADIE helps pick up the equipment and moves to opposite side of stage but she overhears the girls talking.)

CHEERLEADER 1: I never voted for Sadie to be Captain; she thinks she's so cool.

CHEERLEADER 2 *(sarcastically)*: She is always doing the right thing. She is such a goody two-shoes. Kailey, you see it. Don'tcha? Don'tcha?

KAILEY *(hesitant, but wanting to be accepted)*: Uh, yeah- I guess.

CHEERLEADER 1: Let's go before she comes back and wants us to do that cheer- yet again. You coming, Kailey?

KAILEY *(really torn)*: Well . . . OK.

Look back from C1, C2, Sadie

(SADIE begins to cry and sits in a heap. Focus turns to WYATT and ANTHONY talking on the bench.)

WYATT: Hey, there's your dad and mom in the parking lot. Why'd they bring two cars?

ANTHONY *(frustrated)*: Oh man, here we go again! My dad isn't living with us any more, and my parents argue all the time about the dumbest things . . . like who's picking me up . . . and who's taking me to practice. It's driving me crazy!

WYATT: Wow! That really stinks.

ANTHONY: It happens all the time. I just wish things were the way they used to be.

WYATT *(uncomfortable pause)*: Uh . . . well . . . there's my mom. Hey Anthony, hope it works out.

(WYATT exits. Music begins. ANTHONY stays in place as male soloists enters and takes his place near him. Female soloist enters and is near SADIE. Lights narrow to focus on ANTHONY, SADIE and the soloists as they sing the thoughts in ANTHONY and SADIE's minds. See the Director's Notebook [7-65762-16740-7] or the Director's Resource CD-ROM [7-65762-00493-1] for more staging suggestions for this song.)

Questions

Words and Music by
SARAH MOORE and
TIM CONRAD
Arr. by Jukka Palonen

Copyright © 2009 by Pilot Point Music (ASCAP). All rights reserved.
Administered by The Copyright Company, PO Box 128139, Nashville, TN 37212-8139.

PLEASE NOTE: Copying of this product is NOT covered by CCLI licenses. For CCLI information call 1-800-234-2446.

24

What's gon - na hap - pen to - mor - row? What can I do?___

CD: 19

___ What can I say?_____ I have ques -

TEEN FEMALE
optional SADIE

Ques - tions, ques - tions;

- tions, ques - tions, My life___ is up - side___ down;

Up -

CD: 21

CD: 23

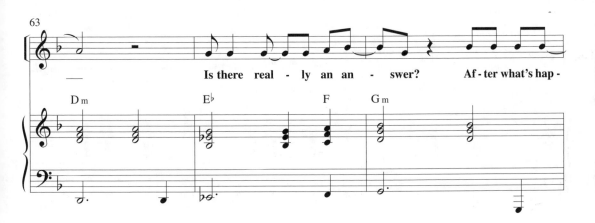

-pened, how can there be_____ a

CD: 24

hap-pil-ly ev-er af-ter?_____ I have ques-

TEEN MALE
optional ANTHONY

I_ have ques-tions._____

-tions, ques-tions, My life_ is up-side_down;

N.C.

Scene Three

(Song ends. Lights down on choir and lights up on WYATT *working on a soccer skill by himself.* COACH *enters after a few seconds.)*

WYATT: Hey Coach, what are you doing here?

COACH: Actually, I was looking for you, Wyatt.

WYATT: For me? Why?

COACH: You know we're going head to head with the Cardinals at the end of the season, right?

WYATT: Yeah. It stinks that we lost against them in that first game.

COACH: Yeah, but we haven't lost since then, and if we continue to play the way we are now, we'll meet them again for the league title.

WYATT *(still focused in his own thoughts)*: If I'd only scored on that pass from Anthony, we could've at least tied the game. I'm sure we'll win next time. That's why I'm putting in this extra practice.

COACH: Extra practice is good Wyatt, but we need a game plan, a new plan to guide us to victory.

WYATT: Well, I have been working on a new move coach, and I'm sure it will work.

COACH: Wyatt, I appreciate your hard work, but I believe what our team needs is to build up more of our players, so they are as confident as you are.

WYATT: OK, Coach. Do you want me to work a little with Anthony, Noah, and Katana? I can meet them on Fridays after school.

COACH: That'll be great, Wyatt, but there's more to the plan. In order for the other players to step it up and become more confident, they can't rely on you the way they have been. They need to depend on their own skills which means . . . over the next few games . . . you're gonna have to sit on the bench sometimes, and let them play without you.

WYATT: Coach? . . . Coach! I have worked hard, so I don't have to sit on the bench. I hate sitting on the bench! I can help the team better on the field.

COACH: Wyatt, I know how you feel, but I need you to trust me as a coach and follow the game plan. It will be for the good the team . . . and you. Think about it Wyatt and I'll see you tomorrow.

(COACH exits)

WYATT *(pacing, thinking aloud)*: How can he say that? Sit on the bench? That's not what I do. How can that be good for the team? I didn't practice this hard just to sit on the bench.

(Music begins. Lights focus on WYATT as he starts his solo.)

Bench Warmin' Blues

Words and Music by
HOWARD DUFF
Arr. by Jukka Palonen

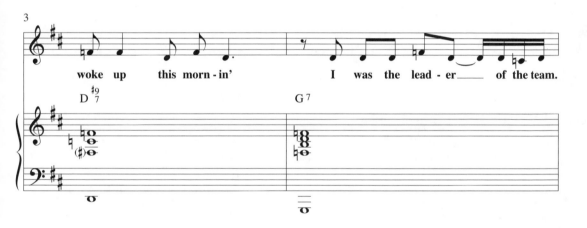

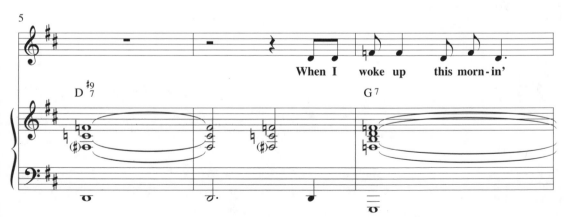

Copyright © 2009 by PsalmSinger Music (BMI). All rights reserved.
Administered by The Copyright Company, PO Box 128139, Nashville, TN 37212-8139.

PLEASE NOTE: Copying of this product is NOT covered by CCLI licenses. For CCLI information call 1-800-234-2446.

36

42

I know the team will lose with-out me and the

D$_7^{\#9}$ G^7

44

coach will know he's wrong.

G^7 D$_7^{\#9}$

46

But un-til that day____ hap-pens

D$_7^{\#9}$ A^7

48

CD: 30

I guess I'm gon-na sing this song.

G^7 D^7

Scene Four

(Song ends. Lights down on choir and lights up on cast. Scene opens a couple of games later. Tigers have won the game, but WYATT is on the bench pouting. As the cheerleaders and the rest of the team come over to COACH, COACH gives kudos to all.)

COACH: All right! That was great! Katana, your defense was spectacular today! Anthony, you really played with confidence in the back third of the field. Noah, waving to the cheerleaders was not appropriate! Give me 5 for goofing off. Everyone count.

KIDS: 1 . . . 2 . . . 3 . . . 4 . . . 5!

(NOAH does 5 pushups or jumping jacks. Everyone cheers when he is done, and NOAH flexes his muscles. WYATT is hanging back and not really participating.)

COACH: Seriously Noah, most of the game you played really well. Could you sense our team working together and getting stronger?

NOAH: Yes sir! Just like you said all season . . . when each of us does our best and uses our strengths, the game plan works better.

KATANA: Hey Coach, the ref needs to talk to you.

COACH: OK, I'll be back in just a minute. *(COACH exits stage)*

(WYATT has sulked back to the bench where the team is celebrating with their after game snack. NOAH notices and confronts him. Others turn and start listening to the conversation.)

NOAH: Hey, what's wrong with you? You're acting like we just lost or something.

WYATT: I wasn't even on the field at the end of the game.

NOAH: So! Our team won. We all can't be on the field at the same time, can we? Coach says everyone needs a chance to play. We've got to be ready in case we're needed.

WYATT: Yeah, yeah, yeah. You don't understand.

NOAH: Wyatt . . . I don't think you understand.

(Lights up on choir as music begins. WYATT and the other soloist for the song stand center stage for the verses that are sung to one another.)

The Choice

Words and Music by
SARAH MOORE and
TIM CONRAD
Arr. by Jukka Palonen

How will you live be - cause you're free?

Copyright © 2009 by Pilot Point Music (ASCAP). All rights reserved.
Administered by The Copyright Company, PO Box 128139, Nashville, TN 37212-8139.

PLEASE NOTE: Copying of this product is NOT covered by CCLI licenses. For CCLI information call 1-800-234-2446.

46

CD: 32 1st time

CD: 34 2nd time

CD: 33 *1st time*
CD: 35 *2nd time*

give up con - trol? This is my life, I make or break

gave it will-ing - ly.___ So you could have___ this choice.

___ it on my own.

What's it gon-na be?___

CHOIR *unis.*

How will you live be - cause you're free?___

52

Scene Five

(Song ends. Lights down on choir and COACH *comes back from talking to the* REFEREE.*)*

COACH: OK, Tigers! Are we ready for next week and the Cardinals?

*(*KIDS *cheer.* WYATT *and* NOAH *high-five each other.)*

COACH: All right, all right, all right! Listen up. Tomorrow is Sports Sunday at my church and I'd love to see all of you Tigers there. Why don't you come, wear your jerseys, and show your team spirit?

KATANA: Hey Coach, what time?

COACH: I teach a class at 9:30 and it would be great to see you there. Then we'll all go to Kids Church together. I hope you can come. I'll see you all later.

*(*WYATT *heads toward* ANTHONY *as team disperses to pick up gear.)*

WYATT: Hey Anthony, you're sort of new to the area. Would you like to come to Coach's class with me tomorrow?

ANTHONY *(hesitantly)*: Well . . . I guess.

WYATT: Great! We leave the house about nine. I'll have my dad swing by and pick you up. See you in the morning. Don't forget to wear your jersey.

*(*WYATT *and* ANTHONY *exit as* SADIE *addresses* JEN.*)*

SADIE: Uh . . . Jen, can I talk to you for a minute?

JEN: Sure. What's up?

SADIE: I don't think I can be the captain of this squad.

JEN: What do you mean? You're committed, on time, and positive. You are THE captain!

SADIE: I don't think the girls like me being the captain. They're stirring up trouble . . . like trying to turn my best friend, Kailey, against me.

JEN: Hmm . . . Sadie, I know you always want to do your best. Right?

SADIE: Yeah, of course.

JEN: Well, sometimes that desire for excellence makes others, who aren't so motivated, feel like they have to put you down in order to make themselves feel better.

SADIE: I just want to do my best, and I want them to do their best, too, but maybe it would be better if I weren't the leader.

JEN: Do you remember the lesson on Moses at church last Sunday?

SADIE: You mean the one where Moses told God he didn't want to be in charge? Boy, I can relate!

JEN: That's right. So God answered his need by sending his brother Aaron to help. God did the same for us.

SADIE: What do you mean?

JEN: He sent the Holy Spirit to be with us always for comfort . . . and wisdom. If you focus on that fact, it will help you to know how to lead and will make it through this tough time. Remember . . . God loves you.

(Music begins and lights focus on SADIE as she sings. Lower lights up on choir as they sing.)

Mighty Is Your Love

Words and Music by
JANA ALYARA
Arr. by Jukka Palonen

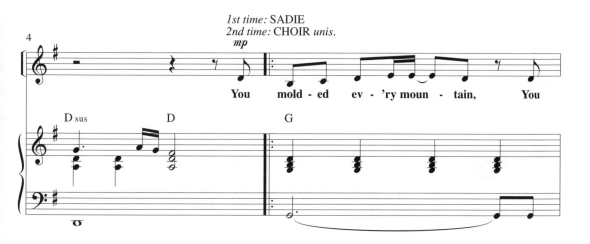

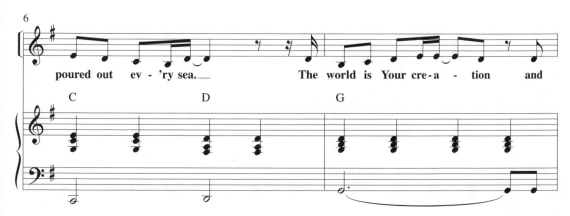

Copyright © 2009 by Pilot Point Music (ASCAP). All rights reserved.
Administered by The Copyright Company, PO Box 128139, Nashville, TN 37212-8139.

PLEASE NOTE: Copying of this product is NOT covered by CCLI licenses. For CCLI information call 1-800-234-2446.

Scene Six

(Scene opens with KIDS dressed in soccer and cheer uniforms. They are seated in a Sunday School class and COACH is in the middle of the lesson.)

COACH: OK, kids, remember . . . Moses didn't feel like he could do the job. Pharaoh was too powerful. The Israelites may not follow him. Moses felt inadequate; he probably stuttered. But, like any good coach, God prepared His team for the opponent. Kailey, do you know how God prepared Moses?

KAILEY: Didn't God turn his staff into a snake?

asks question

COACH: That's right. *(COACH turns to see NOAH playing around.)* Noah, Noah, what else?

NOAH *(surprised)*: Uh . . . oh yeah . . . *(becomes animated)* He helped M-M-M-Moses make the river Nile turn t-t-to blood . . . *(COACH gives "the look")* . . . Then he helped make frogs appear . . . like this one! *(Pulls a rubber frog out of his pocket and scares the girls.)*

COACH: That's enough, Noah! Give me that thing. *(Takes the frog)* But, you're right: God gave him the power to create other plagues. The most dramatic one of all was when He made the angel of death pass over the land. If the blood of the lamb was not on the doorpost of the house, the firstborn child died.

KATANA: Coach, that's pretty mean . . . killing an innocent child!

COACH: I know Katana, but God was setting a plan in place that would free His people and picture the most famous lamb of all, the Lamb of God. In John, chapter 1, verse 29, Jesus was called the Lamb of God. When He died, Jesus paid the price for our sins, so we could live with God forever.

WYATT: Man, God thought of everything!

COACH: You got that right. God is the ultimate coach and His plan prepares us for anything we might face. Jeremiah, 29:11 says, "'For I know the plans I have for you,' declares the Lord, 'plans to prosper you and not to harm you, plans to give you hope and a future.'" All we have to do is to get ready for God to work through us. He wants us to succeed. If we listen to Him and draw upon His power, we can face any opponent!

(Lights up on choir. Music begins.)

On Your Mark

Words and Music by
SARAH MOORE and
TIM CONRAD
Arr. by Jukka Palonen

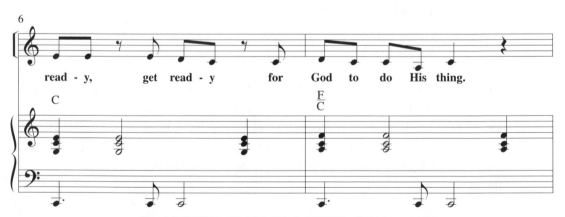

Copyright © 2009 by Pilot Point Music (ASCAP). All rights reserved.
Administered by The Copyright Company, PO Box 128139, Nashville, TN 37212-8139.

PLEASE NOTE: Copying of this product is NOT covered by CCLI licenses. For CCLI information call 1-800-234-2446.

Scene Seven

(Lights down on choir.)

COACH: Hey everybody, its time for Kid's Church. Let's go.

(Everyone leaves the room, but WYATT *and* ANTHONY *remain.* ANTHONY *has picked up the Evangecube.)*

WYATT: Hey Anthony, we've got to go. Kid's Church is going to start.

ANTHONY *(puzzled, holding the Evangecube)*: I don't get it.

WYATT: Get what?

ANTHONY: What's this all about?

WYATT: Let me show you . . . it's all right here. *(Pointing to Picture 1)* The person on the left represents everyone who has ever lived, including you and me. On the other side there is a bright, beautiful, holy light. This represents God. God loves us so much, and wants to be with us, but there is something separating us from Him. We are surrounded by darkness, which is our sin. Sin is all of the wrong things we do in life. God couldn't stand the idea of being separated from His children, so He formed a game plan to bring us back to Him.

(Pointing to Picture 2) His game plan was to send His only Son to live and die for our sins. The Bible says, "God demonstrates His own love for us, in that while we were still sinners, Christ died for us." He was perfect. He never told a lie, He never stole, and He never talked back to His parents. Jesus died up on that cross for you and me. Our sins were nailed there with Him. As He was being nailed to the cross, He was thinking of His children.

(Pointing to Picture 3) When Jesus died on that cross, He was buried in a tomb. A huge stone was rolled in front, and guards were placed there to make sure no one came in or no one came out.

(Pointing to Picture 4) But in every exciting game, there is a great comeback. Jesus was only in that tomb for a short time. On the third day, an angel rolled the stone away, and Jesus rose from the grave. He had defeated death, and gave us all hope.

68

(Pointing to Picture 5) Now here we are again, and we are still surrounded by our sin, but now the cross, that Jesus was nailed to, provides a bridge over the gap to our Heavenly Father. The Bible says, "I am the way, the truth, and the life; no one comes to the Father except through me." But just because the bridge is there it doesn't mean that you are automatically with God. Anthony, you have to choose to take the first step. You have to choose in your heart, and in your mind to believe that Jesus is the Son of God, and to start living your life for Him.

(Pointing to Picture 6) And once you make that decision, God is there ready and waiting to welcome you into His family. You will receive eternal life and your sins are gone forever! All of this is a free gift through Jesus from God, and all you have to do is ask for it. It will be given to you.

What do you think Anthony? Do you want to trust Christ with your life? Let Him be Coach and playmaker of your life?

ANTHONY: Yeah, I do! How do I do that?

WYATT: Just close your eyes and talk to God. You don't have to speak out loud; God can hear your thoughts. Tell Him you're sorry for the things you have done wrong.

(ANTHONY bows his head and prays.)

WYATT: Tell Him that you believe that Jesus died on the cross for your sins and that He rose again from the dead. *(Pause)* Then you ask Jesus to become the leader of your life and make you a child of God. *(Pause)* Then thank Him for making you a part of God's family and the gift of eternal life. *(Pause)* Then you always finish your prayers to God-"In Jesus' name, Amen."

ANTHONY *(says out loud)*: In Jesus' name, Amen.

WYATT: Wow, that's great! Anthony, now all you've got to do is trust God's plan. That doesn't mean that life will always be easy, but it does mean that God will be with you all the way!

(ANTHONY and WYATT exit. Lights down on scene and lights up on choir as music begins.)

Lean Not

Words and Music by
SARAH MOORE
Arr. by Jukka Palonen

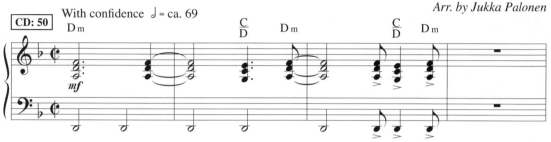

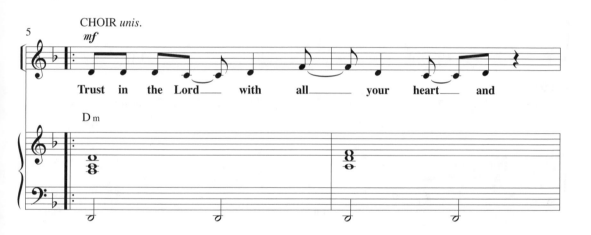

Trust in the Lord with all your heart and

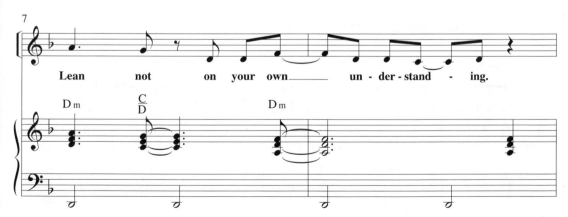

Lean not on your own un-der-stand - ing.

Copyright © 2009 by Pilot Point Music (ASCAP). All rights reserved.
Administered by The Copyright Company, PO Box 128139, Nashville, TN 37212-8139.

PLEASE NOTE: Copying of this product is NOT covered by CCLI licenses. For CCLI information call 1-800-234-2446.

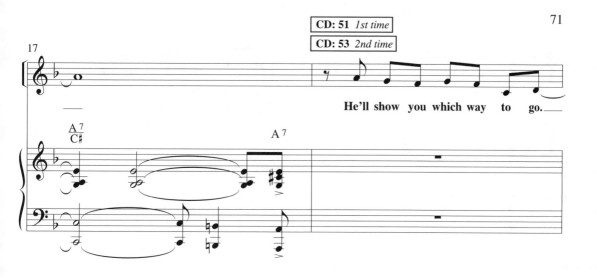

CD: 51 *1st time*
CD: 53 *2nd time*

He'll show you which way to go.

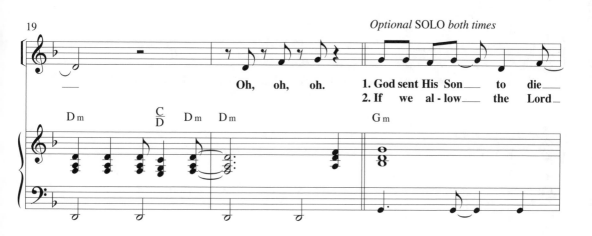

Optional SOLO *both times*

Oh, oh, oh.
1. God sent His Son___ to die___
2. If we al-low___ the Lord

___ on Cal - va - ry. He came to earth___ to set___
___ to lead the way, Lean on His word___ and not___

the sin - ner free. He has a plan,___ a plan___
what oth - ers say. He'll show us how___ to live___

CD: 52 *1st time*
CD: 54 *2nd time*

for you and me and we can trust Him.
from day to day and we can trust Him.

(to pg. 69, meas. 5)

Trust in the Lord__ with all___ your heart__ and

Scene Eight

(Lights down on choir and up on cast. Scene opens in front of the goal. The kids are set up in warm up drills and COACH *is giving them last minute instructions. Focus is on the* CHEERLEADERS. SADIE *is separated from the group doing something with the cheer signs, and the rest of the girls are talking to* KAILEY. KAILEY *leads the group towards* SADIE.)

KAILEY: Sadie, I . . . um, we're sorry we've been mean to you lately. I think you got the idea we didn't want to listen to you, or even be around you for the last few weeks, but you never seemed to get mad.

SADIE: Well, you're right. I felt left out . . . and alone, but Jen reminded me that because I was a Christian, God was with me all the time.

KAILEY: We don't want the season to finish this way. Will you forgive us?

SADIE: Of course, I will. I just wanted us to do our best. I've been praying that you guys would understand. *(Hugs* KAILEY*)* Hey, we better get ready. The game is going to start. *(To all* CHEERLEADERS*)* Come on. Let's practice the Game Plan Cheer one more time.

*(*CHEERLEADERS *set up to do Game Plan Cheer.)*

CHEER TEAM *(cheering)*: Ready? OK! God's Game plan will lead you to vic-to-ry. His way is the best for you and for me!

(Focus shifts to team around COACH *as girls busy themselves with game prep.)*

COACH: Now, listen up team! I want you to know how proud I am of you. We are right where we wanted to be. We've worked hard all season on a game plan to get here. Now it's time to trust the plan. Anthony, remember to stay wide and serve the ball high in the air into the box to Wyatt. Noah, you need to get yourself open as soon as Katana wins the ball. She'll connect with you with an outlet pass. Noah? *(Trying to get his attention)* Noah! Are you listening? This is important!

NOAH: Moses, Coach, Moses!

COACH: Moses?!? Noah, we have a game plan to follow, and we need to stick to it . . .
(Sternly) OK?!?

NOAH: OK, Coach. Sorry.

COACH: Listen up, we're all at a place where now's the time to trust the plan. Wyatt, do
you remember what I said about trust?

WYATT: Yes. trust is never tested unless the outcome is unsure.

COACH: That's right! You don't know what will happen out on that field today. It's just
like in your life. You don't know what is going to happen to you on any given day;
but if you know that God made you and has a plan for you, and you trust that
plan . . . you'll be OK.

(Team exits. Lights up on choir and down on scene. Music begins.)

Trust His Plan

Words and Music by
SARAH MOORE
Arr. by Jukka Palonen

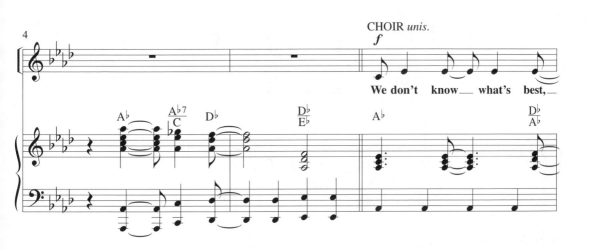

Copyright © 2009 by Pilot Point Music (ASCAP). All rights reserved.
Administered by The Copyright Company, PO Box 128139, Nashville, TN 37212-8139.

PLEASE NOTE: Copying of this product is NOT covered by CCLI licenses. For CCLI information call 1-800-234-2446.

*Cued notes can be played instead of the triplets for this measure.

CD: 58

*Cued notes can be played instead of the triplets for this measure.

8vb

86

Scene Nine

(The song ends. Lights down on choir and then up on scene set up for the final penalty kick of the game. TEAM *re-enters and then huddles together on one side of stage.* WYATT *sits on bench with ice on his ankle.* COACH *is bent over him.)*

COACH: That was quite a hit you took, Wyatt. This penalty kick's yours if you can take it. How's your ankle feeling?

WYATT: It hurts a lot, Coach. I don't think I can do it.

COACH: It's OK. You've played a great game. Anthony can do it. *(To the team)* OK, team. It's tied up, one to one. You've done a great job. We just have a few seconds left. Anthony, we need you to take the penalty kick. Do just like we practiced. Follow the plan. OK?

ANTHONY: You got it, Coach.

COACH: Alright, everybody, Tigers on three! 1, 2, 3!

TEAM: Tigers! *(3 claps)* Tigers! *(3 claps)* Go . . . TIGERS!

*(*ANTHONY *lines up for the penalty kick.* CHEERLEADERS *huddle.* WYATT *is sitting on the bench with his ankle up.* COACH *is beside him. All of the teammates watch anxiously.* REFEREE *blows his whistle.* ANTHONY *pauses and then moves toward* ANTHONY'S *shot goes in. Everyone goes crazy.* REFEREE *blows whistle three times and points to mid-field to indicate the game is over. Lights completely out. Music begins and lights back up full.)*

*(*CAST *takes their bows during the musical intro. They then join the choir for the reprise. See Production Notes for more suggestions for the end of the musical.)*

Game Plan
(Curtain Call and Reprise)

Words and Music by
SARAH MOORE
Arr. by Jukka Palonen

Copyright © 2009 by Pilot Point Music (ASCAP). All rights reserved.
Administered by The Copyright Company, PO Box 128139, Nashville, TN 37212-8139.

PLEASE NOTE: Copying of this product is NOT covered by CCLI licenses. For CCLI information call 1-800-234-2446.

CHOIR *unis.*

We want vic - to - ry; God's got a game plan!

What's our strat - e - gy? Go with the game plan!

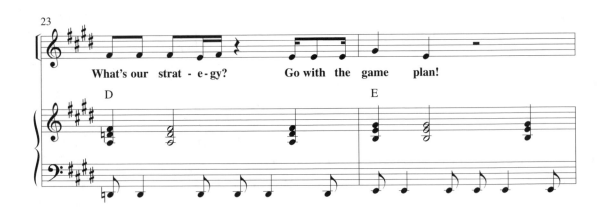

We want vic - to - ry; God's got a game plan!

Production Notes

For more details, tips, choreography and instructions on producing and directing The Game Plan, please see the Director's Resource Notebook *[7-65762-16740-7]* or CD-ROM *[7-65762-00493-1]* and Movement DVD *[7-65762-00513-6]*.

Synopsis

The Sapphire Lakes Tigers have lost their first game of the season to their archrivals the Jersey City Cardinals. The Tigers sports club is facing issues both in their personal lives and on their team. Coach Calhoun has designed a game plan for the team to play better in the final game of the season against the Cardinals. *The Game Plan* includes Wyatt, the best player on the team, sitting on the bench so other players will develop their skills and not depend on him. It throws Wyatt into a state of anger and confusion. Anthony, the new kid on the team, is experiencing family issues at home with a mom and dad separated and decides to let Christ help him through his pain. Sadie, the cheer squad captain, is dealing with relationship issues on her squad. All of them come to realize that God has a game plan for every life.

Casting Ideas

This musical is developed to meet the needs of both large and small choirs. For smaller choirs, the entire choir can become part of the chorus in the bleachers. Larger choirs can feature smaller groups throughout songs. Special parts can be given to each interested child. Coach Calhoun and Coach Jen are the only two adults seen on stage (possible Referee also). Songs can be sung by kids in drama or sung about them by other soloists with proper staging. See more on this under **Song Suggestions**. Kids in the drama should be 4th-6th grade.

Costuming Options

T-shirts with the book logo are available through Personalized Gift and Apparel:

Tom Roland, Owner (888) 898 6172

Website: www.pg4u.com

Email: info@pg4u.com

Or you can download the T-shirt art from the Lillenas website at www.lillenas.com to create your own shirt.

Each child in the production can also be in a royal blue Sapphire Lakes Tigers T-shirt and matching black shorts and soccer long socks.

In Scene 2 and 3, the Sapphire Lake Tigers soccer players can wear a blue and white soccer game jersey. In Scene 3 a few players on the Cardinals will have red soccer jerseys on. Goalie of the Tigers should have a goalie shirt on. Coach can wear a blue polo in all scenes. Coach Jen (Cheer coach) can have a Tigers shirt on with sweat pants. Cheerleaders can have their sleeves pulled up on their shoulders with ribbons or cheerleader clips. Their shorts can also be a little different than soccer shorts, but we don't recommend skirts to keep lengths appropriate. Their shorts might have a white strip on the hem to make them a little different.

Set Design

The story line makes the three scenes very simple to manage. One, you will need to emulate a soccer practice environment with a side of soccer field with a bench area.

Depending on the size of your stage you can add bleachers or risers for effect as well as a snack shack. Soccer goal at end of stage (smaller OK, not regulation).

Second you will need a Church Sunday school classroom. The benches used on the sidelines of the soccer field in Scene 1 can be arranged to simulate a classroom.

Finally, you will need Game Environment where the set looks like Scene 1, but it needs to feel like a game with scoreboard or banners or other things to indicate a game is going on.

Props

Cheer signs with X's and O's depicting a game plan for opening number
Mesh bag for gather soccer balls- used by Noah for Superman gag
Mesh bag for gathering up soccer balls
Some soccer balls for practice
Practice cones for set up of field
Whistles for Coach and Referee
Bible for Coach Calhoun in Sunday school scene- extra Bibles for Closing

Evangecube for Wyatt (go to www.e3resources.com for info)

Rubber frog for Noah

Pompons for Cheerleaders

Game jerseys for Tigers and Cardinals

Microphone Needs

Cordless lavaliere microphones are ideal for drama participants. Hand-held microphones can used for special solos.

Song Suggestion

Some of the solos may be challenging for the children you cast in the show. On the song "Questions," we suggest using teens to do the solos. Then you can stage Anthony and Sadie struggling with the questions they are working through. For instance, Anthony can pace, play with his soccer ball, etc. while Sadie cries, then prays, etc. Or you can completely choreograph Sadie and Anthony if you would like more of a dance feel to this song.

Scene Tips

Scene 1: Coach needs to come off as enthusiastic, likeable leader. Be sure Noah sets the tone for his personality with his Moses/Superman comments.

Scene 2: This is a very heavy scene with issues of rejection for Sadie and pending divorce for Anthony. Be sure to talk your kids through these issues as you practice the drama.

Scene 7: This scene contains the most difficult part in the play because of the length of the presentation of the Gospel. We recommend that that you use the Evangecube pictures projected on screens as Wyatt explains each one to Anthony. If your Wyatt is having trouble with the entire monologue, simplify the presentation but remember to make sure Anthony accepts Christ as Savior. The audience needs to know what happened and how it helped Anthony. This is the most powerful scene of the musical. It sets up the invitation to the audience at the end of the play to accept Christ as their Savior.

Scene 9: Be sure to give some good practice time to the scene that is not scripted for the penalty kick. Instruct the child who is playing the goalie to move to the side as the ball is being kicked so that the goal is made easily. Referee blows the whistle to end the game and the team and choir celebrates.

Closing the Musical: The musical creates a fantastic opportunity for an evangelistic outreach to family and friends. In the play the audience with see how a person can give their life to Christ, just like Anthony did. The pictures of the Evangecube clearly state why Jesus came and why He died on the cross and rose again. The individual decision whether or not to accept the free gift of salvation is stated openly.

It is suggested that after the curtain call and reprise of the song, "Game Plan", that the coach character steps up to the front of the stage and addresses the audience with the offer of salvation. The following is a suggested narrative for the presentation:

"We want to thank you for coming tonight to our musical. In our play tonight you witnessed our character Anthony, accepting Christ as his personal Savior. I believe in an audience like this one tonight there may be people who have not made that decision for themselves.

As you saw in the play, you don't have to say anything out loud: the decision is made in the quietness of your mind and soul. If you humble yourself, ask for forgiveness and believe that Jesus died and rose again for you, He will come into your life and help you face issues that you have to deal with. His game plan for you will become clear. I want to pause for a few moments in silence and let you consider that decision for yourself if you have not already done so. *(Pause)*

Now you saw the Bible I had in my hand in the scene a Sunday School, and we have placed Bibles just like it in the back of the church. If you made that decision tonight and do not have a Bible or would like a Bible to commemorate that decision, please feel free to take one with you tonight when you leave.

Let's pray and then we will celebrate with the cast and crew." (COACH *character prays or pastor comes to lead a closing prayer.)*